Parenting Teenage Boys

How to Form a Bond, Communicate and Listen to your Teenage Son

Table of Contents

Introduction

CONCLUSION

Reviewing what we've learned.

What it means to be a man.

Introduction

Parents of teenage boys don't need to hear it from me that they're doing a yeoman's work.

I know. Teenage boys are a tough row to hoe.

Often inexplicably moody, surly and angry, teenage boys are no picnic. But a parent is there to smooth the road toward adulthood. You may not always understand your budding man, but parents can prepare themselves before the most difficult times arise. They can arm themselves with the right tools to manage the storm before it hits.

Raising teenage boys has a lot to do with anticipating the problems inherent in the project before they arise. There are some common features of the teenage boy that should govern every parent's approach.

One of the most important of these is the hormonal changes they're going through. Hormones are surging through their young bodies, creating conditions which can be confusing, to say the least.

Another is the fact that teenage boys (like teenage girls) aren't playing with a full cerebral deck at this point in their development. This is an important factor we'll discuss in detail, this book.

It's not their fault. They're not being a pain in the butt for the perverse joy of driving you around the bend. They cannot help themselves. Chemical and physical realities compete with social complexities that many of us forget, as we get older.

But we were all young once. One of the greatest gifts you can give your teenage boy is the gift of letting him know you get it. You've been there. You're the adult who has successfully navigated the teenage years, bloodied but unbowed.

Adulthood is the brass ring of surviving these difficult years and your brass ring, concurrently, is the sense of achievement you'll feel in ushering your teenage boy through this challenging period.

The acne. The social awkwardness. The bullying. The sexual awakening. The group think and the desire to fit in. These are all common to the lives of these young people.

Parents need to keep in mind that what may seem a small problem to them is encountered as a catastrophe in the mind of a teen. Demanding that a teenage boy clean his hellishly messy room may seem like a minor matter to you. To that boy, it's a challenge to his autonomy. It's his room, not yours. It's his private space. Your demanding that it be kept to a certain standard may seem not only unreasonable, but *oppressive* when run through the mill of the teenage mind.

In fact, your very presence may seem oppressive to your teenage boy, as he begins to flex the intellectual muscles which will one day be adult independence.

There are days on which you're sure that kid is plotting your early demise (possibly with your cat). He seems to hate you with an incandescent intensity that can set you back on your heels, at times.

But you are still the adults in the room. You are the parents and as the parents, you get to be in charge. But asserting your authority is a balancing act between maintaining order in the face of teenage chaos and putting your thumb down so hard you make matters worse.

Let's talk about how you can form a bond with your teenage son by establishing boundaries and gaining his respect, in this essential guide for parents of teenage boys. We'll also examine a recent teachable moment in the media and how it can help you face-to-face with your teen to underline the values you're hoping to instill in him.

Chapter One: Oh Dear. What can the Matter Be?

Teenage boys can seem like alien life forms when they're in the throes of one of the many crises they're so prone to, during these challenging years.

We look at them and ask ourselves where that sweet, little boy went. Replaced by a surly, pigeon-chested pseudo-adult, we observe his behaviors as though conducting field research on the elusive African gnu, somewhere in a distant savannah.

But the savannah in this case is the home, where the teenage boy roams from the dense foliage of his den to the refrigerator and back again.

We ask how he's doing and he grunts an unintelligible response, head down. Drinking straight from the orange juice carton, he belches as we ask him to please use a glass.

We despair. Despite all our keen observations, the true nature of the beast remains concealed, for the teenage boy is the most elusive animal of all. Straining to understand, our patience is similarly strained by this creature's sustained belligerence.

But why? Why do teenage boys behave the way they do?

Your brain on teen.

Your brain on teen is a wilderness of hormonal activity, all set in the framework of a cerebral structure which has not yet come to full fruition.

If you ever thought there was something wrong with your kid's brain, you're partially right. It's not so much "wrong" as in development.

While your teenage boy may be articulate (when he feels like it) and seems to be intelligent, your teenage boy is also not working with a full set of tools.

Succinctly, teenage brains thinking differently. A recent set of studies, published as a complete volume by the journal *Developmental Neuroscience*, concludes exactly this – that teen brains are very different from adult brains.

The set of 19 studies examined the sources of behavior in teenage boys from the perspectives of neuroscience, psychology and brain imaging. Led by neuroscientist Pradeep Bhide, Ph.D., the team conducting the studies discovered some key differences in the brains of teen boys.

Some of those differences originated in the limbic system (which governs responses to perceived threat). Elevated activity levels in teen boys may explain why emotional responses in boys of this age group are out of proportion to perceived threats.

By measuring brain activity, researchers in the set of studies also discovered that teen boys had almost no reaction to the threat of punishment. In the same portion of the study, it was revealed that they were much more likely to respond to the promise of winning large amounts of money through gambling.

(Is anyone really surprised by this? Not me.)

A molecule, which has been isolated as responsible for healthy levels of fear in situations, which present danger, was also found to be much less active in teenage boys.

The emotionally volatility, carelessness and apparent fearlessness of teenage boys have a chemical root. Add to that root the influence of peers and social messaging through mass media and it becomes somewhat easier to figure out where these guys are coming from.

Making the 20-something connection.
Another aspect of the teenage brain is the connection of the pre-frontal cortex – the part of the brain in charge of problem-solving and making judgements – and the limbic system.

This connection is known to be forged in the early 20s. Teens, in other words have no way of connecting their emotional responses to reasoning and logic. Their emotions are in charge, with a very limited capacity to connect actions to consequences. Without the ability to self-regulate, teenage boys are unable to learn about their emotions and what they mean.

The connection of the middle brain (governing rewards) and the pre-frontal cortex has also not been formed at this point in its development. This makes teen boys more prone to seek out novelty, sex – and drugs. In fact, during the teen years, substance addiction is much more likely to develop.

Add to the all the factors discussed above the fact that your teenage boy's body is producing the male hormone, testosterone, at 10 times the normal rate. This reality is joined by huge outputs of stress and growth hormones.

That's quite a chemical stew going on in a developing human whose brain has not yet developed to a point at which self-regulation is possible. So, if your teen seems impulsive, accident-prone and a little crazy, consider these biological realities and remember – punishment is probably not going to work and may exacerbate an already tense situation.

Now that we've taken a walk through the body chemistry and brain development of the teenage boy, let's talk about how you can help your teen navigate this difficult life transition.

Chapter Two: Being There

Many parents tend to respond to the chaos inherent in the teen years with authoritarianism.   Others tend to the permissive end, allowing their teenage boys free rein to explore and discover.

But both these responses are extreme.   Somewhere in the middle is the sweet spot, where you'll find a basis for forming a bond, gaining your teen boy's respect and establishing the trust necessary in any health relationship.

Silence is not golden.

As boys enter their teens, they tend to express themselves less, preferring silence as the best way to confront their emotions and process them.   Your job is to recognize that silence not as a wall, but as an invitation.

Being there means taking note of subtle changes as well as dramatic ones.   When your teen boy responds to events around him with silence and withdrawal, it's always incumbent on you to let him know you're there; that your love is unconditional and that you care deeply about how he's feeling.

The time to talk to your teen boy isn't when something has already gone wrong.   The "Big Talks" many parents associate with raising boys this age generally revolve around unfortunate events arising from erratic and unacceptable behavior, bad grades at school and managing a budding and lively sexuality.

But when your most profound communicative moments with your teenage boy are when he's disappointed you, he gets the message that you're only interested in offering criticism.

And that can be the foundation for a dysfunctional relationship, in future.   The lines of communication can't only be employed for the sake of correcting problems.   They need to be there to celebrate the person your teen boy is becoming, to share his accomplishments and help him bear his burdens.

If you've ever wondered where emotionally-stunted men come from, look at your teenage boy and ask yourself if you're not creating just such an unfortunate creature, right in your own home.

It's *you* who needs to reach out to *him*. Not the other way around.

Acceptance.

As discussed above, high-quality, intense communication with your teenage boy shouldn't be limited to moments when disciplinary action is being taken. If that's all you're willing to give, then you're creating conditions whereby your son is going to feel inadequate – that he's not good enough. He may even seek attention by repeating past errors, just so you'll criticize him.

It's attention, at least.

Accepting your teen son as he is means letting him know you're proud he's your soon. It means sharing what he values as important and listening to his thoughts about things that matter to him.

Your teenage son wants to be built up, not torn down. Being there to reassure him that he's good enough and that you're enjoying taking the journey towards adulthood with him is daily work. It creates a foundation for further emotional and intellectual development that's solid and dependable.

And that creates confidence and self-esteem. Without coddling him (which a teen boy reads as condescension), you meet him where he stands, letting him know he's "Okay." As a parent, you're acknowledging the difficult reality of crossing the bridge to adulthood and building much-needed trust.

The basis for bonding.

The foregoing two sections add up to the ingredients you need to bond with your teenage son. Talk and accessibility are only part of this project.

Once you've managed to get your son to open up instead of clamming up, numerous opportunities arise to take your relationship to the next level. Fathers especially, are called upon to make an additional effort to bond with their teenage sons, finding as many chances to share quality time with him as possible.

That may mean stepping out of your comfort zone. Single mothers with teenage boys, fulfilling both the motherly and fatherly roles, can do the same. It's not hard to figure out what lights your teenage son up and how you can share it with him.

Keep your eyes peeled for local events you can participate in as a family, or as a father-son, mother-son team. That may be a sporting event, or a music event. If it's music, that's where your comfort zone ends. If your kid likes to hear that band you think sounds like cooking pots being banged together repeatedly, take him to an all-ages event and share the music with him. You may even figure out what the heck he sees in that style of music, whatever it is.

The basis for bonding, as it is with all relationships, is mutual respect. That includes respect for differences and boundaries and that goes both ways. Your teenage son's boundaries count just as much as yours do.

If he has a sign on his door asking that you don't enter, then don't. Even if you suspect something's amiss, violating his trust by breaching his boundaries is going to make bonding difficult. You may be the authority, but you're not an authoritarian regime.

While you're building a bond with your teenage son, don't forget to celebrate the differences. Learn to laugh at yourself. Teach your son to do the same. Moments of laughter are some of the most important you can share with him. They're easily as important as the more serious moments, when you're talking about weightier matters.

The key element in every bonding effort is, of course, your time. You may not have a lot of it, but you have a teenage son who desperately needs to know how much he matters to you.

Make the time. Carve it out. Turn off your TV and go places with him that interest and engage him. Your son needs you to do this. Your time is precious not only to you, but to your teenage son. If you want to get right down to it, your time is his time. He didn't ask to be born and it was you decided he would be. That needs to be honored and lived out as part of the bonding process.

Conquering outdated stereotypes about masculinity.

This is an ongoing project both parents should be participating in. The world would be a much less hostile place if all parents would work with their male children to conquer outdated stereotypes about masculinity.

One of the key stereotypes attached to the social meaning of masculinity is the "strong, silent type". There is nothing strong about being silent. It's in silence that resentment grows. It's in silence that the repression of important emotions (which need to be processed in order not to be become toxic) causes corrosion of the spirit.

Raising a teenage boy to understand that what he feels is valid and important and deserves voice is a gift to both your son and the world he's growing up in. Uncommunicative men are dysfunctional men. Their emotional lives stunted in adolescence, they are the sources of suffering for women, children, friends and co-workers all over the world. Locked up in their own, resentful little worlds, no light penetrates their sullen petulance.

Is that what you want for your son?

No. It is therefore incumbent on you to ensure that open communication is a value in your house. Sharing ideas about what emotions are and how they can be managed with your teenage son is a trust-building exercise that helps him feel less alone. You support him and encourage his emotional growth and resiliency when you give him permission to talk about what he's feeling and experiencing.

Men are not doomed to silence. They are not consigned to a life of repressed emotions and the bearing of feelings which can metastasize when bottled up. By encouraging your son to communicate openly with you, you're building a next generation man who is a complex human, capable of emotional responses which are healthy and constructive.

Teach your teenage son that it's normal to feel things and to talk about them. Teach him also, that the opposite is not normal and a sign that something needs to change. Someday, he'll be a fully-formed adult man who will make a profound difference in his social circles by not being "that" guy.

The next chapter will cover what happens when "that" guy has ascended to a position of power and authority to say things to your teenage son that send the opposite messages.

We're going to examine some problematic features of the now infamous speech of the President of the USA to the annual Boy Scout jamboree. We'll discuss how the speech can be used as a teaching tool by parents of teenage sons.

The message of a swaggering, taciturn, bullying masculinity is in mass media, video games, high school sports locker rooms and even the classroom. Giving your teenage son the tools to question it; to question the norms for what masculinity consists of, is one of your most compelling goals as a parent.

Chapter Three: When the Message Undermines Parents of Teenage Boys

Masculinity is as benign as femininity when it is not soured, or distorted through the lens of resentment and emotions stunted during the teen years. But when it becomes both soured and distorted, it can be corrosive, toxic and highly destructive.

When toxic masculinity takes the reins of power, parents of teenage boys are facing a direct challenge to their efforts to put their boys on the path toward a constructive, healthy life as an adult man.

That's what happened recently, when Donald J. Trump addressed the annual Boy Scout Jamboree.

The Scout Law encompasses the same values parents are diligently trying to impress on teenage boys. I think it's fair to say we all want to raise children who are "...trustworthy, loyal, helpful, friendly, courteous, kind, obedient, cheerful, thrifty, brave, clean and reverent." As an institution, Scouting has traditionally sought to build leaders and good citizens.

And so, when a political leader's speech to a large Scout gathering flies in the face of those values, parents are faced with a collision between the stated values of the organization (and those they hope their sons will model) and another set of values entirely.

As a male authority figure, the President's role in such a scenario is to speak about the importance of community and citizenship and how the values of Scouting create conditions for these realities to be strong and positive.

But that is not what the President did on Monday, July 24, 2017 at the national Boy Scout Jamboree in West Virginia. What the President did on that day was something entirely different.

Unprecedented in the 80-year history of such addresses, the President was unable to offer the gathering anything more uplifting than a litany of grudges and inflated claims about his own popularity. He spoke extensively of himself and his victories, while denigrating opponents and demanding adulation from a large group of hormonally-fueled boys, desperate to be part of something larger than themselves.

In short, he exploited them.

Belonging and exploitation.

Imagine a crowd of 40,000 pre-teen and teenage boys gathered to celebrate Scouting. The President is to speak. The excitement is palpable. The teens in the crowd are emitting vast clouds of testosterone. Most of these boys have never found themselves at an event anything like this.

Instead of creating a positive, uplifting message for these boys, the President politicizes his speech, encouraging the boys to boo the previous President and his opponent in the election which triggered his presidency, last year.

He encourages them to chant the words "I love Donald Trump."

Not "I love the President." Not "I love the USA." The personal adulation the President demanded from a large group of impressionable boys, known to become boisterous in large groups and to ardently wish to be on the same side as the "cool kids," is clearly inappropriate.

Juxtaposed with the selfless message of Scouting's values, the President's politically-motivated and egotistical message completely undermined the stated imperatives of the Boy Scouts – a non-political organization.

Parents of Boy Scouts responded angrily on social media platforms to the address, making it clear they were not only unhappy but furious. All they'd been teaching their sons and the very reasons they'd enrolled them in the organization were effectively undermined by the Leader of the Free World.

The Leader of the Free World.

How do parents respond to such an unseemly display from an authority figure – a daily presence in our lives in a position of almost unmitigated power?

They use the speech as a teachable moment.

Thank you, Mr. President.

Parents all over the USA should be thanking the President right now for providing them with such an overwhelming portrait of the very type of man Scouting is the antithesis to.

They should send him a handwritten note, describing how they used his speech to teach their sons how a man in a leadership role does *not* behave.

The Boy Scout speech stands as a singular, teachable moment that parents of teenage boys can use in their favor. It's a document sited in the current moment which provides a blueprint of what happens when the values you're attempting to instill in your son are either ignored, or not passed on effectively to the next generation.

A son of enormous privilege, Donald Trump's now famous book, *Art of the Deal*, describes a teenage Trump punching a music teacher in the face because "...he didn't know anything about music".

While he did not write these words, he related them to a ghost-writer because he was proud of the incident. He was proud to be a teenage boy with so little self-restraint and so little respect for the adults around him, that he physically assaulted one of his teachers.

One can only assume that he did so in the absence of parents who cared enough about the kind of adult he would become, that they didn't bother to teach him that the entire world was not something he could bend to his will. It's more likely they taught him the opposite.

And I suppose that's perfectly fine if one is born to wealth and privilege. For the rest of us, this is the kind of behavior that begins a life of crime and serial detention in penal facilities.

The Boy Scout speech as teaching tool.

Sharing the Boy Scout speech with your teen boy is an opportunity to share both of your perspectives about what was said and why, in context, the President acted inappropriately.

It's important to teach your teenage boy that thinking critically is key to maintaining an individual read of what's going on around him. Thinking critically about current events is a training ground for your son to think critically about everyday events in his life – particularly those involving peer pressure and the temptation to exploit those around him to impress a group he wants to be part of.

Review the speech. If you're watching online, it's easy to stop and start the video at key moments to discuss the import of the President's words and their effect on the crowd. It's also useful to review the virtues upheld by the Boy Scouts and to juxtapose them against the tone, tenor and content of the speech.

An essential lesson for your teenage boy here is that thinking for himself in every situation is important. When he finds himself in a group of boys, for example, does he move with the pack thoughtlessly, or does he break off because he knows what the pack is doing and saying is wrong?

Another essential lesson is the idea that leadership is humble and applies itself judiciously. A leader is not a "sore winner" who continually rehashes past battles in public. A leader does not publicly hold up for ridicule other leaders, particularly in a setting in which he or she is intended to be modeling the best qualities of leadership.

You will find other important lessons in the content of this speech and they'll be as individual as the relationship you're building with your young man. By reviewing the speech together, you're making it clear to him that you value his thoughts enough to share your own with him.

As parents, you're bringing your teenage son to the adult table to do something uniquely grown up – thinking critically about an event that has triggered an opportunity to interact intelligently about the nature of being a man, a leader and an example for others.

That says a lot about what you think of your teenage son and his ability to exchange ideas and thoughts on a critical level. It's likely that your teenage boy will respond positively and take note of the fact that the discussion is an unusual one.

You're not telling him to clean up his room. You're not lecturing him about sex. You're not criticizing his academic performance. You're having an adult conversation with him about what it means to be an independent thinker, a leader and a positive influence in the world.

That's a huge moment for a teenage boy and one that can make a tremendous difference in the quality of your relationship.

This teachable moment has the potential to build the trust you're seeking. By sharing it and examining it beyond a reactionary, gut level, you're creating a bridge between your man-to-be and adulthood.

You're telling your son that you care about who he is and that you believe he's smart enough and observant enough to have an important, adult conversation. That's empowering for a teenage boy and the lessons inherent in the Boy Scout speech are ones which he'll most likely remember his whole life long.

Chapter Four: Turning Problem Behaviors

You're not magicians and there's no "silver bullet." Your teenage son is an individual who is bound to have a few kinks. All the same, he's one-of-a-kind, so applying blanket strategies is probably not helpful.

More important is the relationship you're establishing and improving by following the advice outlined in this book. A relationship is rooted in what two people know and *like* about each other. It's finding the common ground that bonds people together.

Family relationships are something we can't change. What we can change is our attitude toward what those means. When dealing with teenage boys and problem behaviors which may arise, it's important to keep a few things in mind.

Don't be "disappointed".

No matter what kind of mischief and mayhem your teenage son gets up to, telling him you're "disappointed" is only going to make matters worse.

Especially if you're building a strong bond and a healthy relationship with your son, there's nothing more undermining than expressing disappointment in a behavior. Your teenage boy may have no idea what he's done wrong, or how his actions have disappointed you.

Launching into an expository rant about why you're disappointed isn't going to take the sting out, either. Telling a teenage boy that you're disappointed in him is about the same as saying he "sucks" in his mind (which, as you'll recall, is not yet fully formed).

Be as disappointed as you like. But don't share that information with your kid. Hearing that will only push him away and make him feel like a failure. Remember how much he needs your support and use a different strategy.

Ask questions.

Your kid knows you're not pleased. He knows he's stepped over a line. This could be anything from smoking a cigarette, so getting a speeding ticket, to being suspended from school.

You needn't compound the terror of your teen boy. He's been caught. He knows there's a storm brewing. What he will not expect from you is to be treated like an adult.

That means you're going to sit down with him and discuss the error of his ways, certainly. But you're not going to rant about why what he did was wrong. You're going to ask him all the right questions to get to the root cause of the behavior.

Ask questions like these:

"Did you have any idea that what you were doing was going to have consequences? Did you even think about those?"

It's an honest question. It provides your son with an opportunity to explain what was going through his adolescent mind at the moment he decided to do whatever it was he did.

"What happened right before you decided to (fill in the blank)?"

This is an important question. The response will reveal whether peer pressure and a need to be accepted by the group was in play, prior to the action taken. If you hear that in your kid's response, the right course of action is to talk about why belonging to a group is less important than doing the right thing – even if it costs you friends.

If you have anecdotes about your own teenage years to share, that's even better. What you learned from those anecdotes will demonstrate to him that he's not the first teenage boy to mess up. He comes from a long line of former adolescents who've been there (and survived).

Drugs and booze.

These are big ones, to be sure. Let's not pretend that we all weren't naughty teenagers once and let's not pretend we didn't sneak booze from the parental liquor cabinet, or send some schnook into the liquor store to buy it for us.

Because we did and you know it.

Talking to your teenage boy about substance abuse is an important moment in his life. It's a defining moment. Alcohol is a legal substance, but only for adults. Underage people are not to be near the stuff. They're still growing and dependencies which can ruin their lives can develop quickly.

Opioid drugs may be legal, but they're also highly addictive. Talking to your kid about what they can do is key. This epidemic has taken thousands of lives all over North America and you can help your teenage boy recognize the danger.

As for illegal drugs, well – they're illegal. Getting caught with drugs can mean a permanent blot on a young man's life. Explaining that to your son and ensuring he understands what that means is key.

Not playing the saint, or the authority from above is key to a discussion with your teenage son about drugs and booze, especially if he's been caught in an institutional setting, like school, or even by the police.

Making it clear to your teenage son that you care deeply for his wellbeing is first. After that, sharing stories about how you learned to put substances (illegal and otherwise) in their place tells him you're willing to talk to him about it honestly.

Pretending you're perfect will only irritate and alienate him. While avoiding placing yourself on the same footing as your son, you're being open enough to invite him into a crucial conversation. You're acknowledging that he's ready to have a very adult exchange and to show him a side of you he may not have been aware of before.

Sexual misconduct.

How you manage this is highly individual. Your worldview about sexuality will factor in. One of the most important things you can do, depending on the situation - (Is someone pregnant? Has your son been caught in a compromising position?) - is to impress upon him that sex is normal and that sexuality is inherent to human beings.

You should also be talking about respect for his body. In the same you would talk to a teenage girl about the sanctity of her sexuality, you should be talking to your teenage son about it.

Sexuality is a sacred part of being human which is extremely precious. Talk about mutual respect and responsibility. Ensure your son knows enough about how reproduction works and how to avoid STDs and STIs.

Resist the (no doubt) overwhelming temptation to chastise him, but don't congratulate him, either. You're not high-fiving your kid for breaching boundaries, sexual or otherwise. You're guiding him through the labyrinth of growing up and part of that is being honest and open about sex.

Turning problem behaviors in your teenage son is rooted in the bond you're building and the relationship that bond is founded on. The more you respect each other, the less problem behaviors you'll need to turn.

Chapter Five: But What About Respect?

Respect is a very important thing to many people. You know yourself that when you speak to your elders, your boss and strangers that you show respect and courtesy in order to earn their respect.

Now, as a parent, you also seek some respect from your children but what makes you think that your child doesn't seek respect from you? When raising children in general, making sure that you have their respect is important, but what about you? Even though your son is still a young man, you should know that he still wants to be respected no matter how old he is and if you want to connect and communicate with your son, the key is respect.

People say that one of the most important things when it comes to communication to any relationship, whether it is romantic, friendship, or a parent-child relationship, is respect. When you really think about it, it makes sense. Having a serious conversation with your child isn't going to go well if you do not show that you respect and hear their opinions and arguments. Along with this, it is important that you show your child that respect goes both ways.

Slouching and Grunting

If you have ever sat down to have a serious conversation with your son and only received "the slouch," some grunts and blank stares, then you have probably felt the frustration that comes along with trying to communicate with a teenage boy.

So before we dive into any theories and techniques on earning the respect of your teenage son and him earning your respect, let's have a chat about communication and how we can do this effectively.

When teenagers are being lectured about something they do not want to hear, they often dismiss the conversation. The information goes "into one year and out through the other."

This is definitely a big problem. Obviously, when you are telling your son something, it is usually for a good reason—maybe for his own good or to help him get through something. But giving your advice may be hard if the conversation is just being wasted on a person who isn't even taking it all in.

Here are some good ways to catch the attention of your son when you need him to hear you.

The first thing we should talk about is the idea of lectures. You know yourself that lectures are often boring and embarrassing when they come from authority figures. If you've ever been in trouble for a silly thing you'll know what how it feels. Understanding that lectures are sometimes demeaning is a sure sign that you are making progress.

You have to comprehend that your son doesn't like lectures any more than you do. The difference is that you are an adult and you know how to take these lectures with a grain of salt, heading the words of those who are giving them. Your son, however, is not at that level of maturity yet.

It might be a good idea to ditch the lecture for something else a little shorter and less demeaning. For example, you should compose a short list and let him know that "these are the things you did wrong, here's what you should do next time." This will help in the long run—your child might actually listen to you a little more.

Something else that you can do is to give him food! Yes, it sounds a little odd, but giving your teenage son some food before a good talk is something that you should give a shot. If you are a man, or if you were married to one, you'd know that back in the day they had their fair share of big meals. I know from experience that boys can eat a lot when they are teenagers, as well. So trust me.

Food makes a lot of people happier, too. When you give your child some food, you'll find that their mood might lighten and your words may actually be heard. Next time you want to have a chat with your teenager, do it over his favorite meal. It might get you somewhere.

Don't get mad! As stated before, it may be difficult to control and anger that you might have towards the young man or toward what he has done, but it is important to make sure that you control your emotions. Even if you are not mad and you are upset or happy, you do not want to cry! Crying is a good way to let your child know just how hurt or affected you are by his actions, but it also may shut him out. So you do not want to do that.

If you get mad, it could start a fight and cause a lot of tension between you and him. This could mean trouble, too. You would be bringing yourself all the way back to square one, virtually deleting all of your progress. So, just be careful of what you do and how much emotion that you show when you are speaking to your son.

You should also show that you are on the same team as your child; you do not want to fight. When you show him that you trust him, you are respecting his opinions and ideas. Make sure that you listen to his whole story. This will allow you to really "hear him out" and all for good communication.

Earning His Trust and Respect

When trying to connect with a teenager, it is all about finding out ways to earn their respect and help reassure them that they can trust you. You want to make sure that they can come to you when they need help and they need to be aware of the fact that you are not going to yell or scream at them (no matter how much you may want to).

But how do you connect with your son this way? How do you let him know all of these things without bursting into a lecture about what he should do and how he should do it?

The first thing that you should do when sitting down with your child would be to talk to him as if you have not been in this situation. Some parents do this when they compare their past situations to their child's. Even though this may be good for some teenagers, not all kids are going to connect to that. As they get older, they want to become more independent; they want to be their own person. You might be just trying to help him, but really, you could be fueling an internal fire to be different.

So try to talk to him as if you have never been through this before—even if you have. Ask questions, but not prying questions. You should be making him feel like he is having a conversation with you, it's not an interrogation.

Something else that you could do is show him that you trust him, too. Building trust is a two-way street, so when he sees that you trust him, he will slowly begin to trust you. This could improve your relationship on so many different levels.

Show him that you trust him by going to him when you need help. Maybe you are really busy and you need him to help you do the dishes. You could also confide in your son, letting him in on a financial problem, while asking him to not spend so much money. Follow your conversations with "Don't say anything, though". This will help him understand that you are telling him something that you don't want the world to know; a secret of sorts. Slowly, he will begin to open up to you, as well.

Finally, you should let him learn from his mistakes. A lot of parents make a bad decision and try to keep bad things from happening. The problem is, though, teenagers are sometimes going to run right towards what you do not want them to do! We all know this from personal experiences, movies, and TV shows.

What you want to do instead is to let him go through the experience, as hard as it may be, and allow him to see that it could have been avoided. He may even come to you for advice the next time around. Do not let him do anything that could harm him or others around him; stop him when it comes to that, even if it makes you seem like the bad guy.

Giving him the chance to become independent

Another good way to help you earn the trust and respect of your teen, is to try teaching—and allowing—him to become independent. This can be done in many different ways, one including giving your child a higher curfew or even their own bank account.

This might seem a little crazy when you think about it at first but, depending on the responsibility that your teen shows, giving them a bank account and a monthly or weekly budget to control themselves can help them in many ways! Giving him a budget to restrict their spending will teach him discipline as well as teach him independence in terms of buying his own lunches, snacks, and knick-knacks.

Make sure that you teach your son responsibility, as well. Giving him a bank account does this as well, but you can also teach him responsibility by giving him chores and business to do around the house. This could include doing his own laundry, cleaning his room weekly, or even picking up a younger sibling from school or certain activities. You can also make sure that you set rules for doing home work on the weekdays and Sunday.

When I was growing up, the rule was that our homework was to be done first thing when we came home from school. This way, we had the rest of the night to do whatever we wanted. Explaining it this way might help reduce any fights or disagreements that you may have with your children.

After so long of doing this, your son will understand why it is so important for him to do his homework right away and eventually you will not have to ask! When he gets older, he will no doubt be more independent in doing certain tasks later on in his academic or working life; he will be more responsible in general.

Doing other tasks around the home will also help build your child's responsibility and give him the chance to become more independent.

Independence can be taught by parents through accountability. When your son does something wrong, make sure that he knows that he is the only one that can fix the problem and he has to deal with the consequences. If your child does something wrong, do not lecture him, as we said before. Let him know what he did wrong and tell him what the consequences are. Tell him what he has to do to fix the problem that he has created.

For example, if you have smaller kids, you probably have toys made specifically for those younger children. If your teenager breaks it, you should tell him that he has to use his allowance or monthly budget to pay for a new one! That way he knows that what he did was wrong and he has a good idea of what is going to happen if he does it again.

This is a very simple example, however. Things can get worse when it comes to raising teenagers, but you just have to take it one step at a time. If your child is arrested, for example, for a minor crime—something that he can be fined for. Make him stay in jail for a night before you bail him (if need be) and then make him pay the ticket or work it off if you have to buy it.

All of these things put together should help your child understand the problems that come with misbehaving and help teach him credibility and responsibility, as well.

Allowing your child to experience any kind of labor is another way that you can assure that he is becoming more independent. Getting him to apply for summer jobs, volunteer work, or even odd jobs around the neighborhood will help a lot with many of the problems that we've talked about so far.

When this young man begins to work and he knows that what he does wrong could deduct pay or get him fired, he will understand that his best behavior is most suitable for the workplace. This shows both credibility and responsibility! He will also learn independence and responsibility with his money, as well. The money that your son earns is all his to spend. Hopefully, if you get him a bank account, he would already know just how to spend his money wisely.

Discipline is also an advantage to introducing your teenager to the working world. Showing up on time and following orders and instruction are things that your child will have to get use to no matter who it is coming from. It may be frustrating to him at first and he might complain, but you just have to explain that a lot of people don't like their bosses and you just have to deal with it! Insert some humor in there to lighten the mood and make him smile.

Chapter Six: A Boy Needs Structure

Change and lack of consistency can be confusing for many people. They don't have a routine or the ability to adapt to something, so they just continue and handle any changes as they go.

When a teenage boy lives this sort of life, he could become confused, moody, or resentful due to the lack of consistency. To avoid this, create a structured life for him, setting rules for him to follow, chores for him to do, and things to do around the house when he is home. The idea is to make sure that every day has something that is the same; a routine.

Establishing structure

So, how are we going to actually create a stable, structured environment for a teenage boy? Well, you should start with setting a curfew. Setting a curfew is one of the first things that you should do when your teen becomes of the age to roam the town or city by himself with his friends. This task may cause some conflict with your child and it may not, depending on how late or early you set it.

Determining the curfew for your child really depends on the town or city that you live in and the track record of your child. If your son tends to stay out of trouble (keeping out of the bad parts of town, or not staying out late anyway) then you could aim for a higher curfew, such as 11 to 12 pm, if you wish. We can contrast that with a young man with behavioral problems, you might want to aim for a "punishment curfew": 8:00 or 9:00 pm.

Setting the curfew too early may upset your son and he might try to pull the "You don't trust me..." card, but reassure him that sometimes it doesn't have anything to do with trust, but with how the world works and how dangerous it can be. Your child could just be at the wrong place at the wrong time at some point and get in big trouble. Make sure that you do trust him and that he should trust you too when you say, "It's for your own good".

Establishing structure can also be done when you set certain family days or family vacations. It gives your son something to look forward to during the week. Be careful of what you choose to do on these days, however, as it may be seen as exciting to you or any younger children you have, but your difficult teen may not find it very "cool".

Choosing activities like going to a movie, their favorite restaurants or the water park might be fun. Doing extreme tourism like zip lines, bungee jumping, and more are also great things to consider for vacations.

Having one-on-one time is also important. This will give your teen a chance to connect with you and maybe even open up to you about certain things. Either parent can do this, so if you have a same-sex marriage, are a single parent, or have a spouse working away you do not have to worry about "not being good enough" in terms of a father-son or mother-son connection.

If you can build a good relationship with your son, this helps save you guys from any fights or large arguments, thus creating a peaceful, structured household that everyone can be happy in.

Make sure that when you try to connect with your son, you talk about his interest and yours. This will create balance, and make it seem less like an interrogation.

Speaking of talking, it might be a good idea to let him come to you sometimes. If you do that, it will be easier to get him to talk to you and open up. So make sure that you invest some time every week (or so) into just you and your son!

The most important thing that you can show your son, though, is love. Making sure that he is in a loving home, and making sure that he understands that that is never going to change, is something that you have to do. This is probably the single most important thing for any sort of structure.

Adding trust to that loving home can also help more than you would think. When a child knows that he does not have to lie or sneak around, it means that he doesn't have any stress of keeping secrets. It also saves a lot of stress on you as the parent when you know that your child isn't doing anything that you should be worried about; you can trust him.

Conclusion

Thank you for reading this Essential Guide for Parents of Teenage Boys. Parenting is never easy, but teenage boys present special challenges that must be prepared for prior to adolescence and then met with sensitivity and a strong motivation to build up and not tear down.

Your teen boy is struggling with his identity and his place in the world. You're his guide. Parents are not pulling their sons into the adult world – they're guiding them towards it, with a steady, patient and observant hand.

Building your relationship with your teenage son is primarily concerned with your actions. It's not up to your teenage son to be anything but an adult in formation. It's up to you to guide your boy towards manhood. You are the adults in the room.

You've been through what he's going through (mom too, from a different angle). That doesn't mean you get to project your teenage years onto your son. It means you have wisdom. It means you've faced similar challenges and have information about how they might be met.

Reviewing what we've learned.

In all your interactions with your teenage son, it's crucial to remember what we've discussed about the level of brain development in teenagers. Your teenage son may look like an "almost adult," but he is not. He is struggling with physical and chemical realities over which he has no control.

Acknowledging the differences between the adult brain and the teen brain is one of your most potent tools is developing the kind of relationship you're seeking. Building trust is rooted in understanding and understanding that your teen is still growing and learning is key.

You are the authority in your own home and it's important that your young man-to-be knows that. At the same time, it's important for him to understand that you respect him enough to talk about things that matter and which have an impact on the world around him – and who he will grow up to be.

You now know that your teenage son's brain will not form adult connections until he's already walked into the adult world, in his early 20s. In the meantime, you're there to guide him and support him in his struggles. You're there to let him know he's not alone and to encourage him to talk to you, instead of shutting down.

You are not friends. You are parents. And a parent's role, while it encompasses a certain element of friendship, is not that of a friend – a relationship based on total equality. You are the authorities, but you are benign and loving authorities who are open to all communication with your teenage boy.

You're there for your son when he needs you. You don't wait for the closed door to his room to open, revealing the sullen isolation of adolescence. You knock at the door and make it clear that you're there. Being there is one of the most precious gifts you're giving him. You're telling him that he matters and that you care about what's on his mind.

Your teenage son needs to feel that he's important enough for his parents to take the time to be there for him. This is not coddling. It's simple presence. You're not wiping his nose, ever at the ready with a convenient tissue. You're standing with him and walking with him through the wilderness of hormonally-charged adolescence.

What it means to be a man.

The strong, silent type is a trope which is dying. The "Alpha male"; the blustering, self-important universe-unto-himself, Type "A" male, is also dying.

What is arising in the place of models of toxic masculinity is a man who is secure in himself and who thinks for himself. A man less concerned with conformity than he is with doing what's right. That is the true strength. It's not bullying, self-congratulating, or attention-seeking. It's a human model of "man" which isn't wearing a straightjacket constructed by a world which has made a stick figure of manhood.

Which takes us back to the Boy Scouts. The virtues of Scouting are the true virtues of a masculinity unbound. Freed of his Promethean chains, a real man is a positive influence in the world – a humble leader who brings the best of himself to his family, his community and the world.

Mindful parents will understand that what happens between them and their growing son during the teenage years, is the laboratory in which either a Frankenstein's monster or a towering exemplar of true masculinity will be born.

By building a relationship on trust and respect and by letting your teenage son know that he is good enough to be mindfully guided by aware parents, you're creating a man of the future of whom *you* may be proud and who may, in turn, be proud of *himself.*

Before you go...

Again, I **thank you** for reading this essential guide for parents of teenage boys. As parents, I trust your journey will be a loving one and that the teenage son who challenges you today will become a man who brings the world the sterling values it most ardently craves.

If you enjoyed this book and you thought it will benefit you, I would appreciate it if you would leave me an Amazon review.

Good luck in your journey, I wish you well!

Resources

https://www.psychologytoday.com/blog/anger-in-the-age-entitlement/201306/parenting-teenage-boys

https://www.psychologytoday.com/blog/hope-relationships/201404/9-tips-communicating-your-teenage-son

https://www.psychologytoday.com/blog/surviving-your-childs-adolescence/200907/teaching-your-adolescent-independence

https://extension.illinois.edu/familyworks/teen-03.html

http://living.thebump.com/structure-teenagers-8066.html

CPSIA information can be obtained
at www.ICGtesting.com
Printed in the USA
BVHW040152050220
571486BV00015B/294

9 781975 755355